SMALL LOFTS

SMALL LOFTS

Alejandro Bahamón

COLLINS | DESIGN

An Imprint of HarperCollinsPublishers

HarperCollins books may be purchased for educational, business, or sales promotional use.
For information, please write: Special Markets Department, HarperCollins Publishers Inc.,
10 East 53rd Street, New York, NY 10022

First Edition

First published in 2005 by:
Collins Design,
An Imprint of HarperCollins*Publishers*
10 East 53rd Street
New York, NY 10022
Tel.: (212) 207-7000
Fax: (212) 207-7654
collinsdesign@harpercollins.com
www.harpercollins.com

Distributed throughout the world by:
HarperCollins International
10 East 53rd Street
New York, NY 10022
Fax: (212) 207-7654

Executive Editor:
Paco Asensio

Editorial Coordination:
Alejandro Bahamón

Texts:
Alejandro Bahamón, Sol Kliczkowski

Translation:
Julie King

Art Director:
Mireia Casanovas Soley

Graphic Design and Layout:
Diego González

Library of Congress Cataloging-in-Publication Data

Bahamón, Alejandro.
  Small lofts / by Alejandro Bahamón.
     p. cm.
  ISBN 0-06-083336-X (pbk.)
  1. Lofts. 2. Interior decoration. 3. Interior architecture. I. Title.
  NK2117.L63B34 2005
  747.7'9--dc22
                          2005007821

Printed by: Spain
D.L: SA-646-2005

First Printing, 2005

4|06
4

Introduction

Social phenomena and economic interests gave rise to the typologies of contemporary homes by creating new models of life. Two very distinct trends came about in the second half of the twentieth century as a result of postindustrial processes and information culture. These trends are reflected in diametrically opposed spaces. On one hand is the wish to occupy a large, continual space. Inherited from the occupation of old industrial areas, this trend established the term loft and has led to the creation of surface areas with enormous proportions in which the functions of the house can be distributed arbitrarily. On the other hand, overpopulation of cities has produced a high density in the urban nuclei, which is reflected inside residential spaces through the reduction of the habitable surface area to minimal dimensions. These two trends are juxtaposed, and the result is a typology that–inherited from the process of occupying large industrial spaces–has translated into different types and dimensions that respond to the actual conditions of building in large cities. As a result, the revealing title of this book, *Small Lofts,* brings to light these two contradictory trends, which also complement one another. Lofts such as these make the most of a space's reduced proportions and feature a diaphanous, continual design.

Even though living in lofts was one of the proposals of social urban development at the end of the 1960s, today the loft has been transformed into a product of careful architectural elaboration that few people can acquire. A loft normally means a space between 6,000 and 9,677 square feet inside industrial buildings with various floors and high ceilings between 11.5 and 15 feet. Lofts are generally constructed with solid and noble materials, like brick, iron, wood, or copper. Loft living generated an entire movement, beginning in Manhattan with the recovery of old industrial spaces. Warehouses and abandoned factories in New York City were converted into residences for a certain intellectual elite. This signified a change of direction in the migration toward suburban zones and a resurgence inside the city, which went into full decline after industrial development. The first residents of these spaces were artists and students with little acquisition power and a great need for space. They occupied the interiors illegally and became activists, defenders of an architecture declared obsolete by the industrial sector. The students represented a lifestyle in which art formed part of the daily routine. Soon thereafter, promoters discovered and commercialized the image and the ambience of the artists in order to create an attractive and competitive new product in the real estate market. The loft ceased to be just a space for artistic production and took on a provocative meaning, as an emblem of the freedom of new generations. Today, loft living has become a luxury that few – including many pioneers of the movement – can afford.

The projects presented in this book include the most diverse residential solutions. The spaces all have reduced proportions and conserve the principal design and architectural characteristics of this type of space. In every case, the space had a former use, and rehabilitation started with the renewal of its deteriorated aspect. In general, the former function, as well as the formal existing elements, serve as the project's compositional theme. In most cases, the structural system has been emphasized and incorporated as an important element of the ambience. Some of the common strategies revealed in the book are the conservation of metallic pillars, the elimination of false ceilings, and the cleaning of the concrete or wooden beams. The new finishes generally respond to the home's practical and functional solutions. They are smooth, shiny, and unpolluted surfaces, like stainless steel, glass, or wood, and they contrast with the textures of the materials and the rough finishes of the existing structure. The continuity of space, so typical of a loft, resolves the problem of minimal dimensions. The diaphanous quality of the interior is maintained through ethereal, subtle divisions. Innovative strategies include walls that do not reach the ceiling or the lateral walls, sliding doors that disappear, mobile screens that permit changes in the distribution of the residence, or fissures and translucent

materials that allow light to flow across separated areas. The installations, essential for the transformation of these spaces into habitable places, are often left exposed and used as a theme in the composition. This enables easy access to the system for maintenance and emphasizes the loft's industrial character. Finally, most projects reuse part of the preexisting buildings by recycling some materials and construction elements. This strategy reflects the spirit of the loft, makes the most of its minimal proportions, and reduces the costs of the intervention.

The projects included in *Small Lofts* are all under the minimum surface area considered as a loft, some 6,000 square feet. The book includes projects from around the world, defined by their size, which decreases to surface areas under 215 square feet. These sample projects are equally attractive to architects and designers and to residents of the modern city. *Small Lofts* is a guide that reveals new ways to understand the contemporary loft space.

Alejandro Bahamón

SMALL LOFTS

Flex House

Archikubik

Barcelona, Spain | 1,398 sq. feet | Photographs by Eugeni Pons

☐ This loft was a large space that, thanks to its structural and formal characteristics, offered a range of renovation options. The architect started with the premise of clearing the space and enhancing its features in order to create a residence with flexibility. Archikubik envisioned the loft as a space that could be configured according to the residents' activities.

The architect divided the space into a day zone and a night zone; these zones are separated by the element that constitutes the bathroom: a cube whose walls do not reach the ceiling and that can be integrated into the apartment on one side or the other. This solution preserves the loft's sensation of open space and allows the wooden ceiling beams to remain exposed. The various spaces are divided by panels, mobile containers, and structural pieces of furniture. The fundamental concept is to allow the residents to modify their home according to their needs while encouraging light to circulate throughout. A red panel can either divide the living room into two parts or separate the kitchen from the dining room at will. An element that integrates all the atmospheres, the red panel contrasts with the white walls of the rest of the space. The sliding bathroom doors also contribute to the idea that the space can be opened up and change form.

The kitchen, the closets, and storage space can all fit into a container, making it possible to save space by hiding them. Archikubik designed all the mobile furnishings: the tables, the kitchen modules, and the storage units, which are made out of plywood and finished in aluminum. For the floors, the architect used a smooth concrete veneer in order to emphasize spatial continuity. In order to guarantee privacy between the different areas, the sliding doors are made of natural matte aluminum and security glass, which is glued together using a special adhesive tape.

Based on the idea that residences have different functions, this project analyzes the relationship we have with the spaces in which we live. The resulting transformable, mobile architecture responds to contemporary needs and enriches the home's internal relations.

MOBILITY

The flexibility obtained from mobile elements in this space was achieved using light materials and elements. The work surface in the kitchen can function elsewhere as a desk thanks to its wheels with brakes. The red DM panel can also move around on the metallic rail that runs throughout the space.

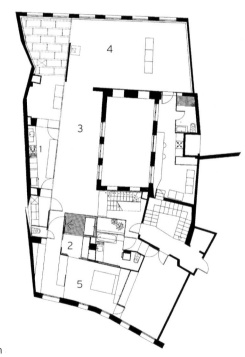

Floor plan

1. Kitchen
2. Bathroom
3. Dining room
4. Living room
5. Bedroom

The panel of DM wood that covers the length of the space is an element of great formal and functional expressiveness. Its movement along a metallic rail alters the relationships between one room and another. It also changes the perception and configuration of the space.

The bathroom is the element that links or separates the social zone from the sleeping area. Inside this box, the details, finishes, and furnishings were designed to merge with either atmosphere.

Sources in Light

Pierre Hoet/In Store SA

Brussels, Belgium | 1,720 sq. feet | Photographs by Stella Rotger

☐ This loft, located in the center of Brussels, was an old leather workshop that the architect Pierre Hoet transformed into a residence. The idea was to create a large open space, maintaining the spirit of the former workshop, while keeping the bedroom and the bathroom private. Hoet not only participated in the renovation of this ground-floor site, but also helped remodel the entire building. His intention was to preserve the original structure of this apartment and to apply the same concept to the whole project.

This apartment has access to a patio with large windows that provide plenty of natural light. The skylight in the ceiling and the windows overlooking the street supply even more illumination. The architect preserved the metallic columns and the ironwork from the leather workshop in order to retain the building's industrial character. Simple materials were used for the renovation. The floors, for example, are covered with holm oak because of its warm and luminous qualities. Plaster panels, painted in light tones like the walls, enhance the exposed cement structure of the ceilings and brighten the space even more. This luminosity highlights the iron pillars and the works of art on the walls. The Boffi stainless steel kitchen, specially designed to fit this apartment without the use of partitions, is incorporated as if it were part of the furniture. The furnishings rely on the nobility of wood to maintain soft tones in the atmosphere. Armchairs grouped around a table define the zones of the living area, the dining room, and the studio. This ample space, divided only to give privacy to certain areas, is envisioned as a whole, but provides a clear distinction between the different functional areas.

NATURAL LIGHT

The design of the metalwork and the distribution of the interior furnishings take advantage of the space's natural light. Toward the façade, which preserves the original structure, a glass covering crosses the space. The patio includes doors that integrate it with the living room and bedroom. The skylight creates a virtual interior patio, which emphasizes all the areas of the residence.

The furnishings avoid design stereotypes and create ambience in every corner, emphasizing the loft's diaphanous character.

Sampaoli House

Claudio Caramel

Padua, Italy | 1,290 sq. feet | Photographs by Paolo Utimpergher

☐ Created inside an old print shop, formerly used as a carpentry warehouse, this loft is located in the center of Padua, in northern Italy. Though the space conserved its original character—the starting point for the intervention—the architect created an atmosphere that more closely matches the typology of a traditional residence. The private spaces are defined by independent bedrooms, but the area that dominates the interior is a large room that groups the functions of the living room, dining room, and kitchen.

The atmosphere of this space is a well-balanced mix of technology and creativity. The result is subtle elegance. The clarity of the forms was achieved through an ingenious strategy to hide certain elements and highlight others. The main entrance is through a garage that leads to the studio or to the residence, resolving the issue of parking while creating an unusual and informal entrance. The space containing the living room, dining room, and kitchen is a large atmosphere bathed in light thanks to large windows and light-colored walls. As in the rest of the residence, traces of its former industrial use are visible, like the brick walls, the exposed tubes, the pillars painted white, and the band of glass blocks in the upper part. The sleeping zone is delimited by walls and doors, as in a conventional residence, and includes two bedrooms and two bathrooms. These interiors stand out for their cleanliness and austere forms. Other highlights are the small-format tiles and the faucets and bathroom fixtures designed by Philippe Starck.

The materials give the space a homogeneous and natural appearance. For the living room floor, the architect used maple wood, while in the kitchen and bathrooms, there is smooth concrete painted with enamel. In some cases, the final white finish reveals the original texture of the brick; in others, it shows a peeled effect. Many of the lamps were designed by the owner. The furnishings, a combination of original historic pieces and recycled elements, constitute the final touch in this detailed space.

DETAILS

The exact measurements of the design details of the interior architecture, and the use of a certain type of furniture inside the space, give this project a somewhat informal and casual appearance, though with truly contemporary taste.

This interior's casual and informal image was achieved through the combination of austere furnishings, pieces designed by the owner of the residence, and some industrial elements, like the metallic bookshelves and the kitchen cabinets.

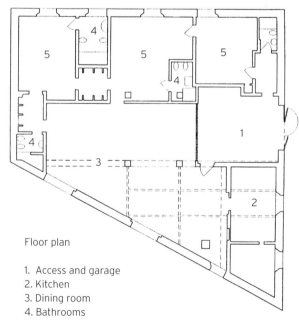

Floor plan

1. Access and garage
2. Kitchen
3. Dining room
4. Bathrooms
5. Bedrooms

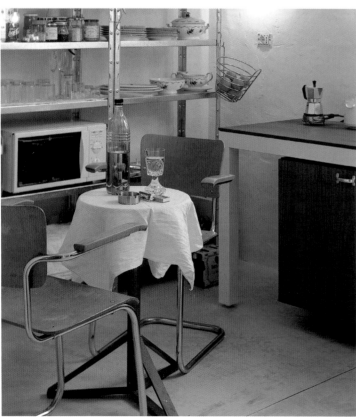

Even though the private zones—the bedrooms and bathrooms—are not part of the general space, they have a similar character. The humid zone of the bathroom is defined by mosaic tiles that cover part of the walls, as if in a drawing.

Formal Unity

Luis Cuartas & Guillermo Arias

Bogotá, Colombia | 1,398 sq. feet | Photographs by E. Consuegra, P. Rojas

☐ This apartment occupies a large part of what was once a traditional residence in a building in Bogotá dating back to the 1930s. Two architects, who collaborate on various projects, decided to remodel the space to create a personal residence for each of them. Architect Guillermo Arias's residence, seen here, was originally made up of several rooms, but it was structurally possible to clear the space in order to form only one room with ample proportions. The starting point for the project was the building's location: close to the city center but on a tranquil and tree-lined street.

Since the apartment is located on the top floor of the building, the architect envisioned an operation that would modify the roof in various ways in order to enrich the space by responding to the different lines of sight. The architect rebuilt the original exterior balcony facing the tree-lined street that had been torn down. The slope of one of the roofs was also altered, generating a longitudinal window in the entire upper part of the apartment that illuminates the back of the

space. Finally, the architect moved the ceiling back in one of the rooms to create an interior patio that leads to the bedroom and isolates it from the immediate neighbors. Next to the entrance are a sink and a toilet, on an elevated platform, hidden behind a curved wall that leads to the main space. Once in this large room, various architectural elements differentiate each zone and give it character. The original chimney was pulled away from the lateral walls and opened on both sides. It now integrates and divides the kitchen and the living room. An axis of rectangular columns is detached from the foyer and demarcates the space for a large bookshelf elevated off the floor. A cabinet containing sound and video equipment indicates the entrance to the bedroom. The two original bathrooms were merged to make one bathroom, with grand proportions and a closet. The design of the woodwork emphasizes the horizontal lines and helps to blend the different zones. The furnishings and the lamps, designed by the architect, unify the formal language of the residence.

FINAL DETAILS

The design and careful elaboration of each piece in this space creates a continuous and harmonic atmosphere. The furnishings, such as the desk that acts as the study and the dining room table, the bed, and the shelves of the kitchen and the bookshelf, adapt themselves to each circumstance while creating a common language for the entire project.

1. Kitchen
2. Second bathroom
3. Dining room
4. Terrace
5. Bedroom
6. Children's room
7. Hall

Previous floor distribution

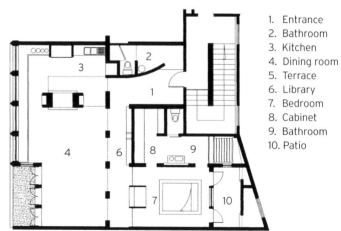

1. Entrance
2. Bathroom
3. Kitchen
4. Dining room
5. Terrace
6. Library
7. Bedroom
8. Cabinet
9. Bathroom
10. Patio

Present floor distribution

The design of the woodwork, for the windows as well as the library shelves, is adapted to the space. The exit to the terrace features large sections of solid wood that give this element solidity.

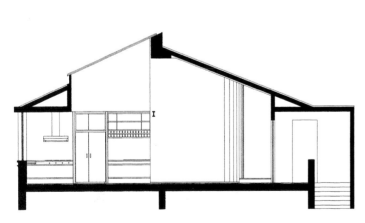

Transversal section

All the kitchen utensils are exposed, and the shelves were designed according to their function. Under the stainless steel counter is a line of boxes, adapted with the woodwork design.

The floors, made of wood tablets, were preserved from the original residence, but treated with natural dyes to create a darker color.

A Continual Path

Luis Cuartas & Guillermo Arias

Bogotá, Colombia | 968 sq. feet | Photographs by Eduardo Consuegra

☐ This project, together with the previous one, forms part of an integral reformation that the two architects carried out on an old building in the center of Bogotá. The architects transformed the space into their personal residences. This particular project occupies the part of the building that previously contained the kitchen and the dining room.

Both projects share certain qualities, including the structure of the building and the tree-lined setting. On one hand, these circumstances inspired similar operations in terms of alterations to the roof, an opening toward the tree-lined street, and the clearing of the interior space. On the other hand, each architect's distinct needs and architectural concepts brought about very different living spaces. After demolishing the existing walls, the architects envisioned the location of the new pieces that make up the residence. The goal was to create a continual space with diverse relationships between the different areas, and a circular, continual path that covers the entire residence. After crossing the entryway, the circulation offers two alternatives. On the left side, a table extends all the way to the door and invites entry into the kitchen. On the right side, a corridor containing a large bench and a bath integrated with the chimney leads to the living room, which features unexpectedly high ceilings. From here, a steel stair leads to a walkway where there is a small studio linked to a terrace. The chimney is open on both sides and paves the way to a more intimate zone with shorter ceilings, which opens onto the balcony and overlooks the tree-lined street. After crossing the bedroom and the closet, the path ends, arriving once again at the kitchen. An elevated platform under the kitchen and bathroom conceals the installations and enriches the relationship between the spaces. The materials define the character of each zone. In the entryway, the smooth, painted cement floor continues until a wood dais in the more intimate area replaces it. The walkway creates an aspect of lightness, while the walls that make up the interior give a sensation of solidity. The mixture of textures and surfaces make this residence a rich space with a continual path.

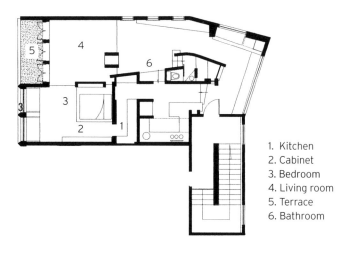

1. Kitchen
2. Bathroom
3. Dining room
4. Terrace
5. Bedroom
6. Children's
   bedroom
7. Hall

Previous floor distribution

1. Kitchen
2. Cabinet
3. Bedroom
4. Living room
5. Terrace
6. Bathroom

Present floor distribution

TEXTURES

The great formal expressiveness of each corner of this interior is accentuated by the different textures achieved through the careful mix of different materials. Concrete, green marble, brick, wood, steel, and glass combine harmoniously to give each space its own personality.

Due to the apartment's interior configuration, the path crosses all the spaces, allowing the resident to enjoy each atmosphere while making the most of the dimensions.

The disk-storage cabinets and the bookshelves form part of the interior architecture. This careful design emphasizes the play of surfaces and textures.

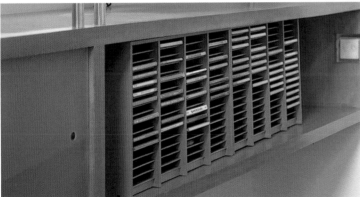

Taking advantage of the apartment's location on the top floor, various operations were carried out on the roof. A skylight in the kitchen, located in the center of the apartment, permits this space to enjoy natural light.

1. Living room
2. Studio
3. Terrace

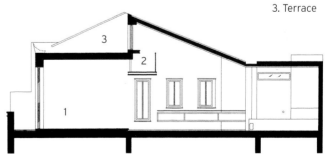

Transversal section

Loft in Islington

Caruso St. John Architects

London, United Kingdom | 806 sq. feet | Photographs by Hélène Binet

☐ This house and studio are located in the neighborhood of Islington, in the northern part of London. Though the neighborhood is traditionally residential, the loft is situated in an old, two-story warehouse. The building was constructed in different eras and suffered from the various additions and renovations. The project's starting point was the formal unification of the structure through a single "skin." Another task was to appreciate and revive the space's constructional and functional past.

The project's goal was to create a space in which the existing elements merge with the new ones in the same formal language. For the renovation, the architects used modest materials like chipboard wood, panels of plaster and cement fiber, and insulating glass. All the materials were used in their natural state, avoiding superimposed claddings, so that their material presence resembles that of the preexisting factory and preserves the industrial atmosphere. The old brick walls are exposed and treated like a smooth surface, which the architects re-covered in some places. Through this mix, the architects created an ambience that avoids temporary and stylistic references.

A new front of insulating glass hangs over the original brick façade of the warehouse. The glass resembles a silk screen on which the shadows and openings of the interior are projected. The composition varies according to the hour of the day or night, creating different effects on the interior and exterior of the residence, where the façade becomes a true urban lantern.

In the back zone of the roof, the architects incorporated a skylight that permits the entrance of natural light through to the ground floor. Diagonal forms break the rigidity of the interior geometry, and the two floors, which share a basic language, are connected by a staircase.

AUSTERITY

The clear and clean atmosphere of this space was achieved by carefully controlling the degree of intervention in the old space. The new furnishings, such as coverings and finishes, are reduced to a minimum.

The element added in the upper part, which is perceived as a box superimposed on the original structure, consists of a light structure that amplifies the interior proportions of the space and collects natural light through two large windows.

1. Kitchen
2. Living room
3. Dining room
4. Cabinet
5. Bedroom
6. Bathroom
7. Empty

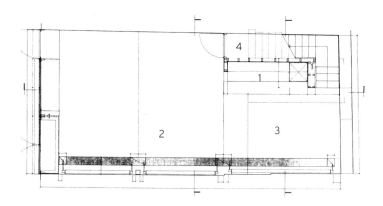

Ground floor plan

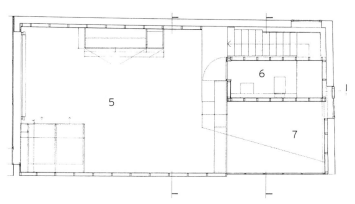

Attic floor plan

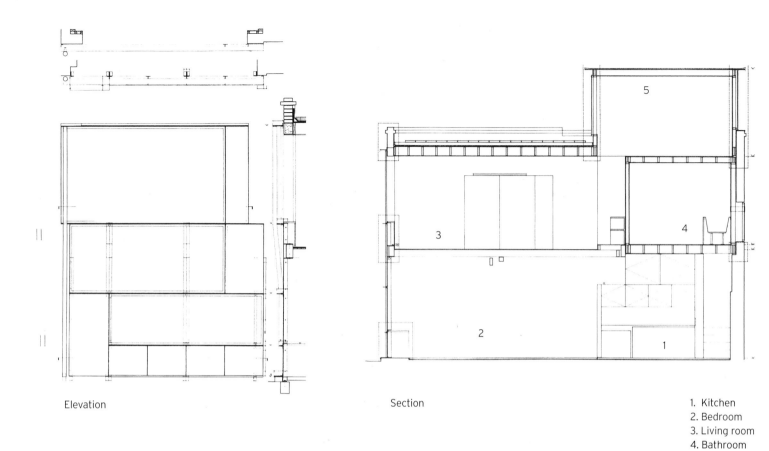

Elevation

Section

1. Kitchen
2. Bedroom
3. Living room
4. Bathroom
5. Skylight

The floating layer of steel and glass is a curtain superimposed on top of the original brick façade. This layer solves the openings in a systematic way and creates a homogenous image that relates to the construction's industrial origin.

Translucent glass creates a large surface through which natural light can enter. It also provides privacy from the immediate neighbors.

Spatial Relations

McDonnell Associates Ltd.

London, United Kingdom | 1,290 sq. feet | Photographs by Carlos Domínguez

☐ This apartment, located in the center of London, was originally a structure without a ceiling that the owner wanted to remodel into a place where he could escape from the hustle and bustle of the city. The best features of the space, natural light and splendid views from the windows, are emphasized in this renovation.

The project's main challenge was to give the apartment mobility, so that the lighting or the structure of the atmospheres could be altered with little effort. To achieve this goal, the architect used light elements that are easily maneuvered. The solutions include curtains that diffuse the light, a pivoting, horizontal door that separates the kitchen from the dining room—inspired by garage doors— and another vertical door that separates the living room from the staircase. The staircases and the living room are linked by a revolving wooden door with an axis in the center that turns 360 degrees, making it a decorative object that enriches the space. The stainless steel kitchen provides an industrial feel, and can become part of the living/ dining room thanks to a panel that can be raised and lowered. The mixture of different materials, according to the characteristics of each space, enriches the overall atmosphere. The second floor is reached by way of glass stairs that allow the light to filter through. On the top floor, we find the bedroom, the bathroom, and a small living area that is connected to the lower floor with a metallic staircase. In contrast to the glass and metal, the wood flooring unifies the entire space. For the bathrooms, the architect used slate on the upper floor and marble on the entrance level. Wood covers the doors and some walls, giving the atmosphere warmth. Various mirrors generate a sensation of open space. In both bathrooms, there are built-in sinks of matted glass with classic fixtures. Glass closets lighten the space. In this London apartment, the diverse materials and the relationship between the different areas, which can be modified according to the layout, generate a functional home with spatial richness.

PIVOTING DOORS

The wooden door that leads from the staircase to the living and sleeping areas has a pivot in the center of its frame, producing a double entrance. The stainless steel door that divides the kitchen from the dining room can be adjusted to restrict or increase the opening between the two spaces.

Stainless steel materials and the color white were chosen to reflect the light and to enhance the sense of open space. The bathrooms include materials such as marble, slate, glass, and mirrors that, through their placement, create optical effects that amplify this small space.

Roof under Roof

Barbara de Vries & Alastair Gordon

New Jersey, United States | 1,183 sq. feet | Photographs by G. de Chabaneix

☐ This loft is hidden in the forest, at the edge of a canal in New Jersey. A fashion designer and a journalist/writer discovered the building, an old, abandoned brick factory, and decided to remodel it into a place to live and work. The clients wanted to preserve certain elements and adapt them into their new home: the industrial style, the brick walls, the immense windows, the open ceiling, and the cement floor.

For the renovation, they constructed a large loft out of wooden sheets that create an intimate space inside the bigger volume. Metallic pieces support the wooden structure, which looks like a house inside the house, dividing the space while maintaining the original atmosphere. The loft, a platform reached by way of a wood and aluminum staircase, houses the bedrooms, the designer's workshop, and a bathroom. A recycled laundry room and its fixtures contribute to the home's antique character. The small living area of the loft is separated from the other bedrooms with panels of birch on rails, so that the space can be enlarged or closed off at will.

The variety of furnishings creates the warmth of the ambience: a large leather club chair, an armchair upholstered in white cotton, a Windsor chair, an African bench, and a ceramic table from the 1950s. The designers hung large photo negatives against the large windows and mosquito netting above the bed, which is isolated from the wall by a wooden panel. The spare use of furnishings further emphasizes the industrial aspect and the sensation of open space.

The industrial kitchen was ordered from a restaurant distributor. To create a more intimate and warm atmosphere, the designers used pieces of furniture and natural materials. The wood bookshelf occupies a wall of the office while the ambiences of the kitchen and office are separated with translucent panels. In this way, light from the large windows bathes every corner of the space.

MEZZANINE

The addition of a wooden structure inside this old factory respects the original industrial style and creates a comfortable residence. The loft amplifies the space and creates a more intimate atmosphere. Separated from the existing walls, the loft is like another piece of furniture.

The furnishings include old, recycled elements, which are treated like design pieces. The furniture complements the space's mixed character, which includes pieces of wood, leather, stainless steel, and plastic.

The loft enjoys natural light that enters through the windows and from below. This is especially important because the structure is isolated from the perimeter of the space. Sliding doors link the various rooms of the loft. The fixtures and the recycled bathroom fittings combine with certain antique decorative pieces to establish a dialogue with the space's rural character.

Loft in Plaza Mayor

Manuel Ocaña del Valle

Madrid, Spain | 1,613 sq. feet | Photographs by Alfonso Postigo

☐ This project involved an irregularly formed apartment in an old building located in the center of Madrid. The structure was disorganized and had suffered significant damage and numerous patchwork renovations. The load-bearing walls were wide and presented variable strokes. The passageways were badly defined, and there were angles and projections that made it difficult to move around in a space with such great depth.

The architect restructured the space by creating a regular and orthogonal order. He reorganized the circulations in a space fragmented by sustaining walls that are important structurally and also to organize the space. The new distribution divided the loft into two large zones: an open one for the primary living space and another, with similar dimensions, that was broken down into smaller areas. A criterion for the renovation of these spaces was to respect the structural elements, since the overall state of the building was poor. The circulation was reorganized so that the resident can appreciate the space as a whole. The materials and textures used for the remodeling reflect the concepts of the apartment's new structure. Woodwork was eliminated in order to free the apartment from the weight of its surroundings. Woodwork and metallic veneers for the furnishings and the doors were used to waterproof the humid zones. This project strengthened the role of the load-bearing walls. Not only structurally functional, they also organize the space. An irregular series of opaque and thick dividing panels gives the loft a new spatial distribution.

TRANSPARENCIES

The relationships between the different spaces, the bedroom and the study or the TV room and the living room, are achieved with transparent elements, such as glass, or a simple curtain that can divide each zone. The decorative palette, in light tones, also unifies the space and emphasizes the feeling of spaciousness.

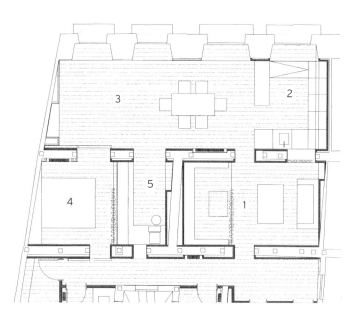

Floor plan

1. TV Room
2. Kitchen
3. Dining room
4. Bedroom
5. Studio

Even though some elements of the original space were preserved, such as the dark wood platform, new materials transformed the character of the space by giving it a contemporary image. Designer furniture, like the chaise longue by Le Corbusier upholstered in courtide, complements the atmosphere.

The stainless steel table, which serves as a counter in the kitchen and as an informal dining room table, is a folding sheet attached to the wall that makes for continuity.

The openings in the walls create relationships between the various areas of the residence, such as the TV room and the kitchen. The openings also take advantage of natural light to illuminate the spaces in the rear of the apartment.

Optical Illusion

Gil Percal

Paris, France | 1,075 sq. feet | Photographs by Gilles Gustine

☐ Before architect Gil Percal renovated the space, this apartment in the third district of Paris consisted of various spaces on the fifth and the sixth floors of the building, without any communication between them. Percal created access to the upper floor, uniting the two levels and gaining space for an additional room, increasing the surface area by 463 sq. feet. The project's focal point was the union of the two levels via a monumental staircase that occupies the entire entrance to the apartment.

In the renovation, the architect sought to take full advantage of the natural light from the windows and their views of Parisian monuments. A studio on the fifth floor leads to the sixth floor via the staircase that contains a blue element in the center. This item is the hidden support of the upper floor, concealing a metallic column on the left side. The aluminum texture of the stairs and the geometric play between this element and the staircase creates an illusion of reversibility that alludes to drawings by M.C. Escher.

The sixth floor is the setting of a large and unified space that includes the bedroom, the kitchen, and the bathroom. The area containing the living room and the dining room is structured around the wooden ceiling frame that is asymmetrically laid out and preserves its original state. The kitchen is mounted on a dais and separated from the main space by a wall only 23 sq. feet long. This piece of furniture, on the side of the living room, is used as a large bookcase to store, among other things, audiovisual material. The bathroom and the bedroom are located on the other side of the apartment, along with a large closet paneled in chipboard wood with stainless steel fittings. The wood floor, the white walls, and the lighting contribute to the apartment's warmth. This upper-level apartment also benefits from the light of the peripheral windows and skylights.

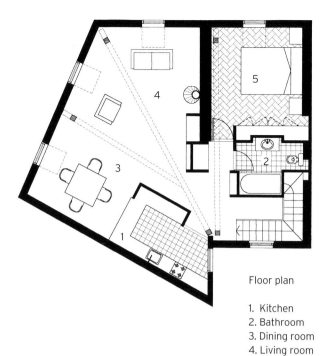

Floor plan

1. Kitchen
2. Bathroom
3. Dining room
4. Living room
5. Bedroom

The texture of the metallic veneer contributes to the desired optical effect and creates an antislip surface. The same material is used to line the closet doors in the auxiliary room.

GEOMETRIC PLAY

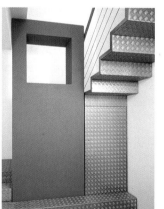

The staircase does more than resolve the structural and functional elements of the project. It also creates an attractive and fun volumetric play that entices the visitor. The cubic forms and the relations between them are more pronounced due to the innovative use of color and light.

73

For the closet doors in the main bedroom, the architect used sheets of chipboard, which are in plain view, to showcase their texture. The space is enriched by antique decorative pieces and the wooden structure of the ceiling, which was incorporated into the interior.

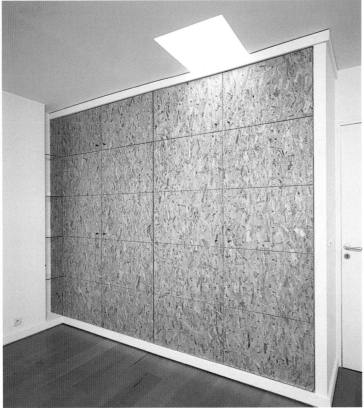

Four Atmospheres in One

Hugh Broughton Architects

Gloucestershire, United Kingdom | 968 sq. feet | Photographs by C. Domínguez

☐ This house was constructed at the beginning of the twentieth century, and its eighteenth century Palladian façade was transported on roads specially constructed for the project. The former dance hall, located at the southern part of the house, was divided in the 1920s to create a series of smaller rooms with low ceilings. Hugh Broughton Architects renovated these rooms by restoring their original characteristics and adding new, contemporary components.

The original space was reorganized to accommodate the different areas of an individual residence: living room, bedroom, closet, and bathroom. The architect raised the ceilings, demolished the unsightly chimney ducts, and remodeled the windows in order to restore and consolidate the space's original character. Various architectural elements were then incorporated into pieces of furniture, to allow for total perception of the space. The different areas are divided with modules placed perpendicularly to the residence's main axis. Each one contains, respectively, the closet, the sink, the shower, and the shelves that serve as the headboard of the bed and bathroom unit. By freeing up the space and adding few furnishings, the architect created the desired sensation of amplitude and spatial continuity. The architect specially designed all the furnishings for the space, achieving harmony throughout the residence. The white walls and glass contrast with the furnishings made of dark wood, including the bathtub and the front part of the sink. The bathroom zone is defined by pieces of stone that contrast with the existing wood floor. The fixtures and lights built into the false ceiling reinforce the project's characteristics and adapt themselves to functional needs. Halogen lamps are used in the bathroom—aligned in the same direction as the modules—while reflectors illuminate the ceiling of the living room for mood lighting. Two fixtures function as reading lights in the module at the head of the bed. Hugh Broughton Architects managed to preserve this home's classic atmosphere by maintaining the white walls and the wood floor. However, the overall space features new elements that give it a contemporary and functional air.

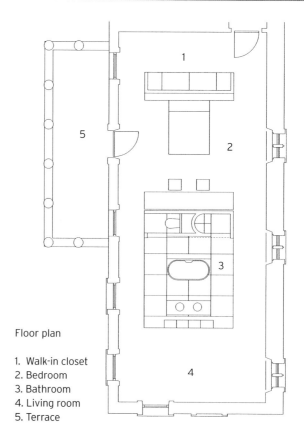

LIGHT MODULES

The modules that divide the space are made of light, easily constructed materials. Nevertheless, they have a solid appearance thanks to their forceful forms and the white tone that meshes with the existing architecture.

Floor plan

1. Walk-in closet
2. Bedroom
3. Bathroom
4. Living room
5. Terrace

The dark wood furnishings contrast with the floor, which is the color of the original parquet recovered from the house.

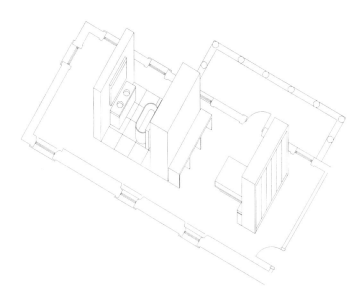

Axonometric perspective

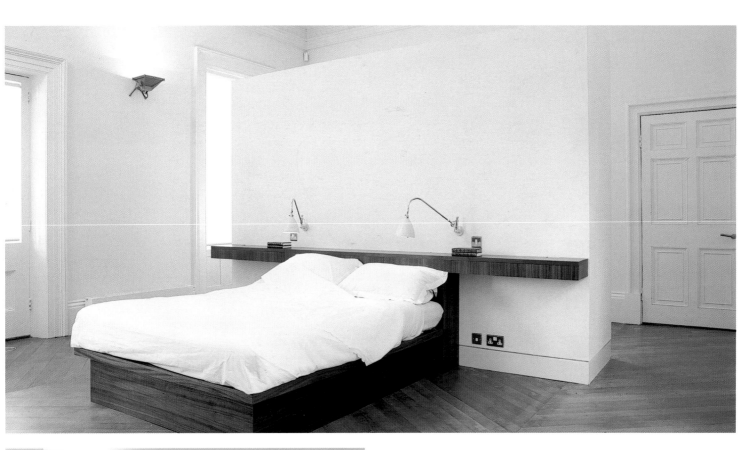

The lighting, built into the false ceiling as reflectors or as fixtures in the interior modules, supports the distribution and creates diverse spatial qualities.

All the bathroom and heating appliances are incorporated into the interior modules, emphasizing the clean geometric lines. The furnishings adapt themselves to each area and fuse with the general space.

Basic and Functional

Project Orange:
Christopher Ash & James Soane

London, United Kingdom | 753 sq. feet | Photographs by Jonathan Pile

☐ This building on Banner Street in London was an old factory that was transformed into apartments years ago. The shape of the space determined the interior distribution. The idea was to give each space natural light, while dividing the bedroom area from the living zones with two very different spatial characters.

The residence is organized along a hallway from which one accesses the private areas: the bedroom, the bathroom, and the studio. The hallway ends at a large social space, which combines the living room, the dining room, and the kitchen in one atmosphere with ample proportions. This distribution makes the most of the generous light from the windows while creating diverse settings without the need for divisions inside the space.

The combination of hardwood floors, the sliding door of the studio, and the white walls adds warmth and complements the industrial atmosphere of the original structure. The architects conserved the brick-bearing walls that strengthen the apartment and establish a relationship with the exterior of the building.

In terms of furnishings, the architect wanted to maintain the amplitude of the space by using only essential elements. The furnishings mix design and contemporary models with the simplicity of an old armchair or a recycled seat. The kitchen cabinets are made of wood in order to complement the floors and create a unified look. To give clarity and the impression of cleanliness, the two kitchen tables are white and in the same light tones as the bathroom. The lighting of the apartment begins with some halogen lights built into the false ceiling of the hallway that continue to the large space at the back. In the kitchen, the architect used lamps with more diffused light, and a floor lamp illuminates the living room.

This project managed to integrate the spirit inherited from the factory with all the necessary elements for a residence. This London loft makes the most of the luminosity from its large windows.

LIGHT-COLORED WOOD

By unifying the material of the elements, the architect integrated the diaphanous space of the living room and its different components. The light wood of the floor is repeated in the kitchen cabinets and in the sliding door of the studio, creating one type of "skin" that covers the space.

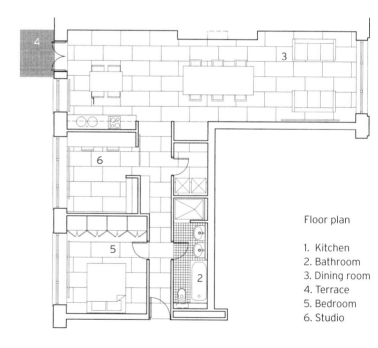

Floor plan

1. Kitchen
2. Bathroom
3. Dining room
4. Terrace
5. Bedroom
6. Studio

In order to give the space the character of a traditional residence, a space in the kitchen was extended toward a small terrace that was previously used as an emergency exit. The interior furnishings also accentuate the traditional style. The bathroom features light colors and rectangular tiles that complement the brick walls in the rest of the space.

One Space inside Another

Alexander Jiménez

New York, United States | 753 sq. feet | Photographs by Jordi Miralles

This loft has a rectangular layout and is situated in an old factory building in an industrial neighborhood in New York City. The goal of Alexander Jiménez´s renovation was to maintain the industrial feel of the space, yet adapt it to provide modern comforts. In order to establish different zones, the architect used functional and constructive solutions that avoided having to break up the space with walls.

The extensive renovation focused on preserving the original atmosphere of the space. Jiménez restored the original brick walls and wooden beams, but the floor had to be replaced. Walls were put up only to separate the bedroom and the bathroom. The kitchen, bedroom, and bathroom are contained in a structure with a false ceiling that gives the area warmth and leaves an empty storage space. The frame contains all the electrical, water, and heating installations.

The kitchen remains open to the rest of the house, and partition walls are used only to close off the bathroom and to conceal the bedroom. The living room and the dining room are located in the same space, yet two atmospheres are created by placing separate rugs under the furnishings of each space. Natural light pours in from the large exterior windows and gives the loft a sensation of spaciousness. The oak floors create a warm and unified look. Sofas, a kilim rug, and black leather and steel armchairs by Le Corbusier are located around the chimney, situated on one of the lateral walls in the living room. An oak table and some Thonet-style chairs made of curved wood distinguish the dining area. The kitchen contains a refrigerator and a work island, illuminated by the recessed lights in the false ceiling. In the bedroom, clothing suspended from a steel bar gives the space a transitory character.

The harmony of this loft was achieved by adapting each piece of furniture and each object to its practical and aesthetic function. Its efficient proportions and distribution help to characterize the overall atmosphere.

LUMINOUS BOX

This box, made with light lines and plaster panels, delimits the service zone. Painted bright white, the panels reflect the light from the windows, creating a bright space inside an area with tall, dark-brick walls.

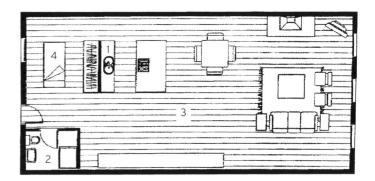

Floor plan

1. Kitchen
2. Bathroom
3. Living room
4. Bedroom

The kitchen, custom-built in the same tones as the wood floor, acts as an element that both relates to and divides the living area and the bedroom.

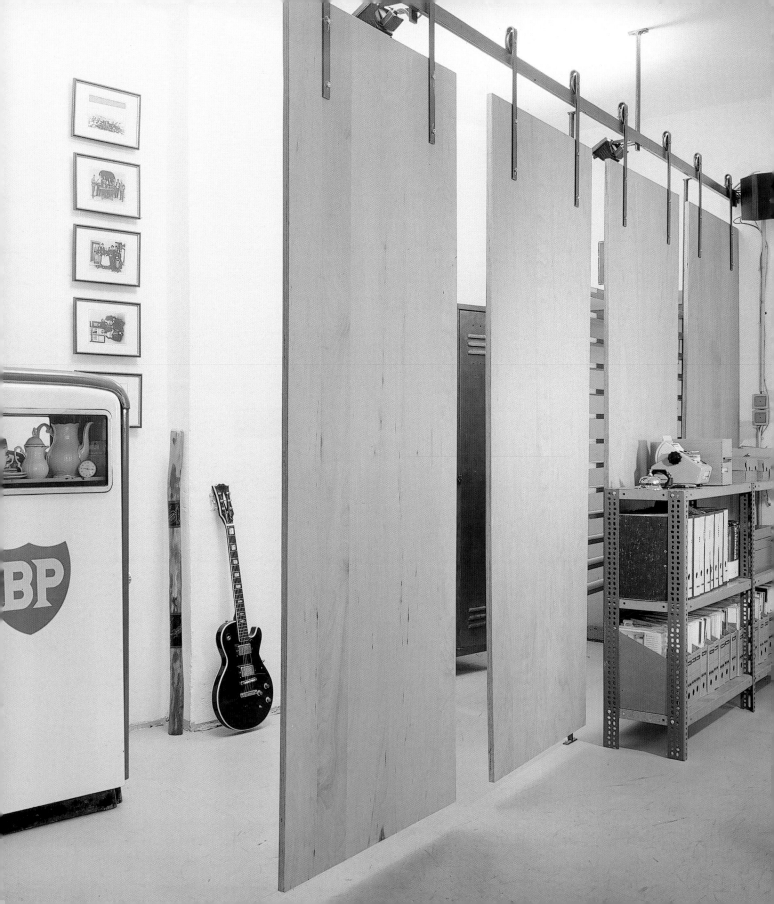

Flexible Integration

Siggi Pfundt/Form Werkstatt

| Munich, Germany | 806 sq. feet | Photographs by Karin Heßmann/Artur |

☐ Located in the center of Munich, this apartment forms part of what was previously a sewing machine factory in the city's old industrial area. The German architect renovated the space as a private residence. The project had three goals: to give the space flexibility, to preserve its original character, and to employ basic, easily constructed materials and methods for the renovation.

In order to divide the apartment, the architect installed five modular chipboard wood panels that hang from a metal rail. These elements accentuate the longitudinal axis of the unit and separate the private and social zones. As a result, the bedroom—differentiated from the rest of the environment by its wood floor—can remain isolated from the living room and work area, or it can become part of the large open space. The social and work zones are grouped in the longitudinal sense along the façade in order to make the most of the space's only source of light. The circulation of the panels along the rail gives the space structure. The panels also control the flow of natural light toward the most intimate part of the residence, located at the back. This visual division conserves the apartment's sensation of amplitude and its dimensions.

For furnishings, the architect used industrial pieces of furniture found in informal stores and souks, like the recycled gas pump used to store the dishes or the office filing cabinets used to store clothing. An old freight elevator found on the site was incorporated into the wall as a shelf. The cement floor alludes to the industrial spirit of the old factory and mixes with the wood and metal to create warmth in this factory-turned-apartment.

The ingenious and flexible use of panels preserves the apartment's continuity and characteristics as much as possible, while resolving the practical considerations, all within a modest budget.

MOBILE PANELS

To maneuver the panels with ease and give the renovation a warm image, the architect opted to use birch plywood. Since the panels are attached only to the upper part, metallic platens are used as reinforcements. They give the elements rigidity and support.

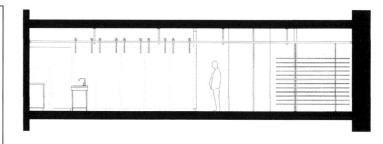

Longitudinal section

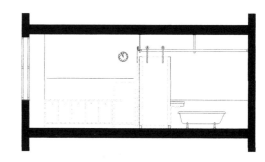

Transversal section

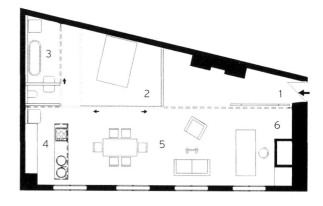

Floor Plan

1. Access
2. Bedroom
3. Bathroom
4. Kitchen
5. Dining room
6. Work area

The façade, defined by its transparency and industrial character, was important to the interior design. The private zones, located at the back of the residence, have privacy thanks to the mobile panels that avoid the use of curtains covering the windows.

The central table, in the same tone as the birch plywood panels, blends with the warm-toned furnishings to create a cozy environment that preserves the characteristics of the industrial space.

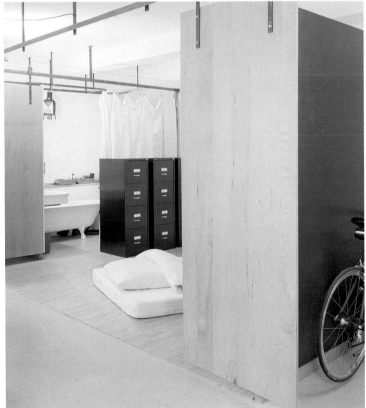

Organic Lines

Antonio Fiol

Majorca, Spain | 753 sq. feet | Photographs by Stella Rotger

This 753-sq.-foot apartment is located in the center of the city of Palma, on the island of Majorca. It was a typical old apartment until the refurbishment project transformed the space into a conventional residence with spatial continuities. Priority was given to the access of light in the back part of the space. To achieve this goal, the architect created open and linked spaces that are both functional and formal.

A play of volumes and organic lines runs throughout the apartment, unifying the different elements in a single language. The omission of an entrance hall permitted direct access to the central space. The entrance separates itself from the kitchen with an irregular-shaped table, which contains a built-in faucet and kitchen sink. Adjoining this first space is the living room, in which the architect constructed a platform of cement attached to the wall that serves as the base of the sofa. The kitchen leads to a platform that had previously been an interior patio and is now the location of the built-in, tiled bathtub, which prolongs the

table's design of curved lines. A horizontal glass opening with an inscription links the bedroom and the kitchen, taking advantage in both spaces of the light that shines into the bathroom. The apartment defines itself through its different levels and types of flooring.

There are few furnishings, since the principal elements are already incorporated into the architecture. In the entrance, a bookshelf designed by Ron Arad continues the undulating character. The kitchen units are from IKEA and the floors are floating parquet of natural cherry-wood. The division of space is established through the links of three objects that emanate from the floor: the kitchen table, a base on which to sit, and the bathtub.

The white walls, the open spaces, the transparencies, and the exploitation of light contribute to the sensation of clarity and amplitude. Yet, the characteristic that enriches this interior the most is the way that light filters from one space to another, without comprising the character of each environment.

INCORPORATED FURNITURE

A good part of the furniture, including the dining room table, the bathtub, and the living room sofa, form part of the interior architecture. Built during construction, the table and the sofa are finished with smooth cement, and the bathtub is covered in tile. The geometry of these elements, in curved forms that break the rigidity of the space, also relates them to one another.

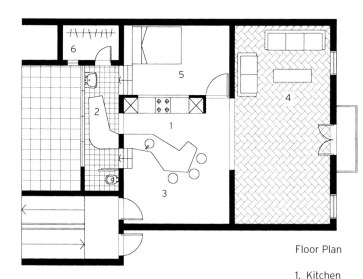

Floor Plan

1. Kitchen
2. Bathroom
3. Dining room
4. Living room
5. Bedroom
6. Cabinet

Simplicity, reflected in the materials, the finishes, and the furnishings, is the main characteristic that achieved this fresh and relaxed atmosphere.

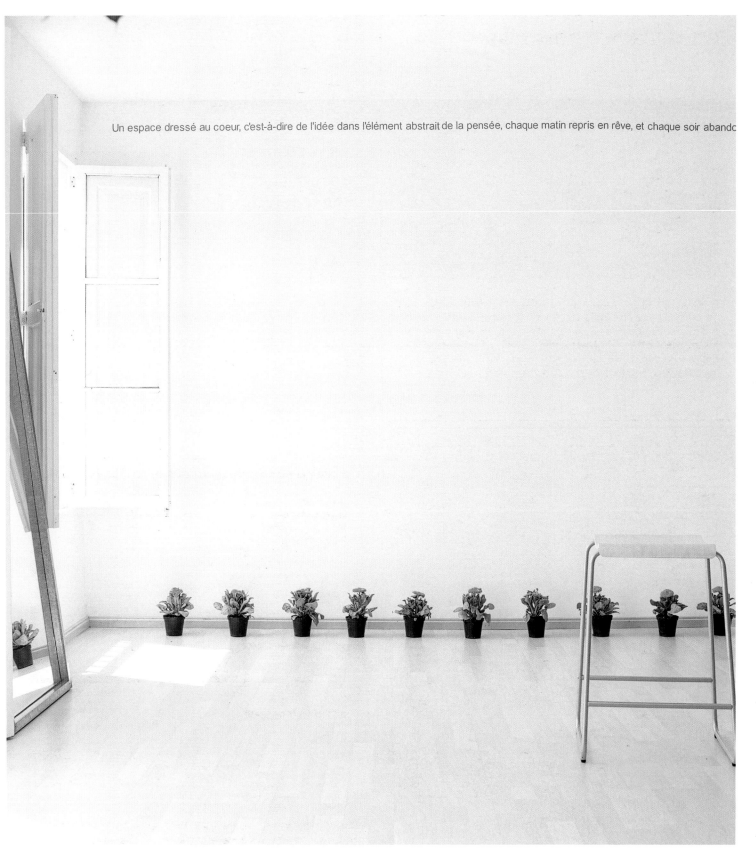

Un espace dressé au coeur, c'est-à-dire de l'idée dans l'élément abstrait de la pensée, chaque matin repris en rêve, et chaque soir abando

En Architecture, j'aime la simplicité; de même, en cuisine.

Vegetation forms part of the interior design and is incorporated into the architecture itself. Flowerpots are placed in the extremes of the cement sofa and frame the ambience. In the dining room, a small hole acts as a bud vase.

The integration of shelves in openings in the walls, fissures, or glass accentuates the blending of the space while allowing natural light, which comes from the two extremes, to flow throughout.

En Architecture, j'aime la simplicité ; de même, en cuisine.

103

Loft on Trafalgar Street

Carles Bassó & Cristian Cirici

Barcelona, Spain | 753 sq. feet | Photographs by Stella Rotger

☐ This small apartment is situated in a building that was completely remodeled to house both residences and small offices with similar characteristics. The project's basic objective was to enhance the building's industrial image. Despite the fact that the building was once used as a garment factory, it had a series of architectural elements that seemed more appropriate for a residential building.

The architects decided to strip as much of the remaining structure as possible, in order to discover the industrial heritage of the building's twentieth-century past. They exposed the forged iron pillars, the steel beams, the tie-beams, and the arches formed by the partitions. New elements such as the hallways, the doors to each apartment, the staircases, the elevators, and the lamps were selected from a repertoire of industrial constructions.

The apartments are formed by only two rooms: the kitchen, which is open and located in a corner, and the bathroom, which is the only closed space. The architectural plan is slightly elongated, and light pours in from both sides of the building. One of the sides is the façade overlooking the street, while the opposite side is a translucent glass gallery that houses the entrance.

The strategic form of the bathroom divides the large unitary space into two areas: a more intimate space next to the façade looking over the street, and another, more public space close to the entrance with the services and the kitchen. The bathroom itself is also separated into two zones, so that the washroom is an open area flanked by a partition wall made of glass blocks. The architects attempted to leave as much open space as possible. The kitchen is located close to the door and next to the bathroom. Parts of the kitchen—the refrigerator and the washing machine—are integrated into the same space as the bathroom.

The walls and the partition walls are plastered and painted white. Parquet covers the floors of the primary space, while light-colored tiles are used on the bathroom floor and walls. In the bathroom, a large, side-to-side mirror over the sink gives a sensation of openness in a reduced space.

BASIC MATERIALS

The interior character of these spaces was achieved by exposing the raw materials of the building. The metal beams and vaults of the upper partitions are on display. Also visible are new elements like the dark wood floor, concrete blocks that divide the apartment, and metallic cross sections that form the windows and doors.

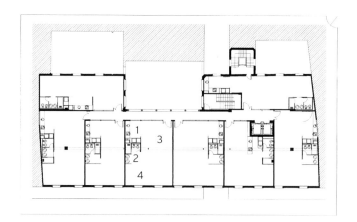

Floor plan

1. Kitchen
2. Bathroom
3. Living/dining room
4. Bedroom

For this intervention, the architects rescued structural elements from the building, including the vaults that supported the partitions and the concrete block walls, and incorporated them into the interior of the residences.

TRAFALGAR 38-46

Elevation

Light shines in from the central patio, where the entrance to each apartment is located. To make the most of the light, while preserving the intimacy of the residences, the architects recovered the façade in matte, white glass.

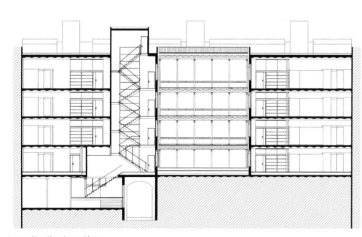

Longitudinal section

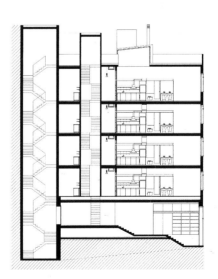

Transversal section

The stainless steel sink reflects the same geometric language as the rest of the space. On the lower part of the washstand, a door opens to reveal a small storage space.

Courtyard

François Muracciole

Paris, France | 753 sq. feet | Photographs by Morel M. Pierre/ACI Roca-Sastre

☐ This old workshop is situated at the end of a small patio in the popular Belleville neighborhood of Paris. A young photographer and her husband commissioned the architect François Muracciole to transform the space. Since it was an old mechanical workshop, the rooms were somber, with chipping walls and industrial objects that were incorporated into the new design.

The project entailed converting the space into a comfortable, well-lit dwelling. The idea was to take advantage of the elements that contributed to the space's original character and alluded to the workshop that was once located there. The patio, located in the center of the space, was hidden by a plastic ceiling. By eliminating this ceiling, the sun illuminates the entire space, including the bedrooms situated in the old warehouse. A large window overlooks the patio, and a loft functions as a guest bedroom or as a TV room. When the patio is opened during the summer, the living room becomes an open-air space.

The furnishings include objects recycled from the post office or from the workshop itself, including a lamp by Christophe Delcourt and a chair by Charles Eames. Muracciole designed the staircase that leads to the loft. This unifying element measures 7 feet high and 16 inches wide and is made of solid iron tubes varnished in a matte finish. The steps, with 6 inches between them, are made of wood, matching the parquet stained specifically for the restoration. All the objects and the details of the finishes help preserve the spirit of the former workshop.

The great challenge of this project was to conceive a habitable space from an old workshop. The result is this apartment of recycled space and furniture, whose charm suggests its former use.

METALLIC CROSS SECTION

The doors and windows, as well as the interior of the loft and the staircase, were made with metallic cross sections to maximize the entrance of light and enhance the original character of this space.

The actual use of the space, as well as the decorative details, alludes to the original character of the mechanical workshop.

Inspired by the recycling of objects, this space features tables, chairs, shelves, and mirrors that clearly reflect the owner's desire to maintain the space's original industrial appearance.

Space for Two

Guillermo Arias

Cartagena de Indias, Colombia | 860 sq. feet | Photographs by Carlos Tobón

☐ This small, recreational apartment designed for a couple occupies what were once two living rooms in a 1930s building in Cartagena de Indias. The building is located in Santo Domingo Plaza, one of the most emblematic spaces in the city. Despite the apartment's splendid views of the plaza and the church, the interior was run-down, and divided by a confusing and disorganized series of exposed beams.

The first step was to reproduce the atmosphere that most likely existed in the original space, but with a contemporary feel. A series of large moldings define the general space, which is now continual and free of dividing walls. Various architectural elements make up the different areas and disguise the central column that forms part of the structure. Just beyond the entrance is a space that contains the kitchen, dining room, and living room. This area ends with a window overlooking the plaza. The kitchen is designed as an isolated table that contains all the appliances and also functions as the dining room table. A low wall, with an incorporated bookshelf, connects this space to the bedroom. A sliding door made with strips of wood and interfacing also makes it possible to divide the areas. The bathroom is found in back of the bedroom. The headboard of the bed separates the bathroom from the bedroom and also functions as a closet. A double sink defines the bathroom's social and private areas. The toilets feature the same symmetry as the sinks, and there is a central shower. Almost all the details of the furnishings are incorporated into the interior architecture. The architect, Guillermo Arias, designed most of the furnishings himself, including the shelves, the marble countertop in the bathroom, the kitchen cabinets, and all of the lamps. Arias is well known for his details that enrich this small space and give it formal unity.

VOLUMETRIC PLAY

The transformation of this apartment into a single atmosphere with diverse functions was resolved by creating different spaces that relate to one another and define the functions of the residence. The moldings, low walls, horizontal planes, and niches were carefully studied to create aesthetic and functional harmony.

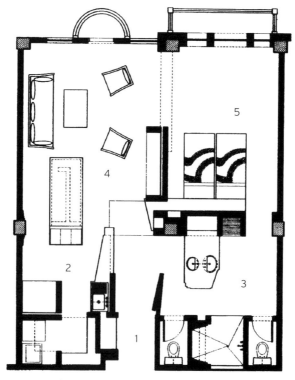

Floor plan

1. Access
2. Kitchen
3. Bathroom
4. Dining room
5. Bedroom

The false depth of the walls creates a dialogue with the original, spacious character of the apartment. Niches used as shelves are incorporated into the architecture itself. The lamps, designed by the architect, feature bronze, antique crystal, and alabaster that allude to the space's original, classic style.

Horizontal Unit

Stephen Quinn & Elise Ovanessoff

London, United Kingdom | 645 sq. feet | Photographs by Jordi Miralles

☐ This apartment is located on the first floor of a typical four-story Georgian house in the neighborhood of Marylebone in central London. This project entailed remodeling the first floor, which was originally a reception. Previous renovations were of poor quality, so the architects decided to re-create the original space and adapt it to a new, more efficient use.

The apartment consisted of two different atmospheres connected with some steps. The architects first restored the large room at the front to its former size and moved the kitchen to a more convenient location. The bedroom is located in the back and leads to a walk-in closet with a sliding door painted with green and blue stripes. The bathroom was carefully designed to accommodate all the necessities. The bed is made of wood and has four drawers below that complement the closet as additional storage space. As a result, the bedroom is uncluttered and gives the sensation of open space. The furnishings in the large front room have dark tones. A desk of lacquered wood and four black chairs define the dining room, and the living room includes an armchair in the form of an "L" with white cushions surrounding a low table. The walls are white and all the decorative elements are limited to objects, sculptures, and statuettes placed on top of tables.

Certain elements, such as the chimney and the large windows, refer to the spirit of the old house. A key feature of this project is the use of space and light, which, combined with the high ceilings, transforms this small apartment into a modern and practical home. The sparse use of color mixes with the solid, dark floors to create contrast.

The finished interior of this small loft still has traces of the original Georgian house built 200 years ago. Nevertheless, the architects have managed to create a completely modern apartment with comfortable and practical surroundings.

TWO COLORS

Dark tones are used for floors, tables, chairs, and everything else that makes up the low part of the space. White is used for all the walls, cushions, and textures of the upper part.

Floor plan

1. Kitchen
2. Bathroom
3. Dining room
4. Closet
5. Bedroom

The small tiles with light separations between them create an interesting texture that adheres to the same color palette as the rest of the residence.

Morton Loft

Lot/Ek

New York, United States | 645 sq. feet | Photographs by Paul Warchol

☐ This old apartment, located in New York's West Village, was situated on the fourth floor of a building used for parking. The characteristics of the space—high ceilings and a regular shape—required a division of the functions and a special effort to preserve the residence's spacious character.

The project entailed separating the private areas from the rest of the space with an object inside that is a throwback to the apartment's past. The architects decided to encapsulate various zones in two tanks used to transport gas. The tanks contain the most intimate functions of the residence, leaving the rest of the space free as a social and living area. One of the two modules is laid out horizontally, and hangs over the living area. Inside, it contains two sleeping podiums. Two hatches on each side of the tank, connected to hydraulic pistons, can be opened with a switch to ventilate and shed light on the beds. The second container is found in a vertical position and occupies the entire height from the floor to the ceiling. It houses two bathrooms, one located on top of the other. A system of railings and resin in the walkway leads to the loft, to the bathroom of the second floor, and to the beds. This enabled the architects to take advantage of the high ceilings and to leave the first floor clear.

For the furnishings, they used the same industrial language with which they conceived the interior intervention. The primary materials are metal for the furniture and a continuous enamel pavement for the floors. By using cement and leaving the electrical and gas installations exposed, the architects enhanced the loft's flexible and industrial character. Warm colors, like the red of the tables and chairs or the yellow of the beds, contrast with the cold tones used for the renovation.

For this New York loft, an industrial language informs the layout of the space, along with the materials and finishes. The result is a habitable residence full of originality.

INDUSTRIAL CONTAINERS

The use of gas transport tanks inside the space required the adaptation of these elements for domestic use. In the tank that contains the beds, the architects cut out ventilation grilles, incorporated hatches, and adapted a horizontal platform. In the tank that contains the bathrooms, they installed the bathroom fixtures and created an interior partition to divide the space into two levels.

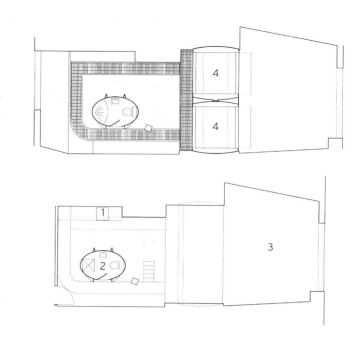

The color contrast between the blue pavement, the red furnishings, and the orange interior of the upper tank enriches this space by creating interesting focal points.

Floor plan

1. Kitchen
2. Bathroom
3. Living room
4. Bedroom

The system of compartments installed in the tanks gives privacy to the sleeping zone and conveys an image of advanced technology in the residence.

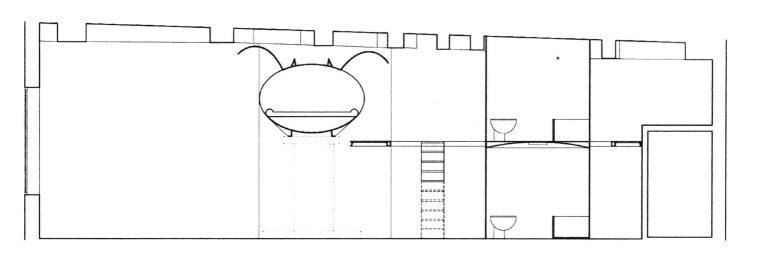

Section

Two Atmospheres and a Box

Mónica Pla

Barcelona, Spain | 645 sq. feet | Photographs by José Luis Haussman

☐ Before it was renovated, this old apartment, located in Barcelona's Ciutat Vella quarter, featured lots of rooms and little natural light. The deteriorated and neglected space was transformed with the goal of creating a luminous and spacious residence in just one environment.

The first step was to tear down various walls and to open up, frame permitting, a variety of windows so that natural light could flow in. Even though there were no walls to separate the space, the designer managed to provide intimacy in the bedroom and to differentiate between the kitchen and the living area. To separate the bedroom from the main room and still maintain spatial continuity, designer Mónica Pla placed the bathroom between these two spaces. Accessible from the bedroom, the bathroom contains a shower and is contained in a box with partial walls. The sink, mounted on one of the exterior faces of the box, is completely integrated into the bedroom space. The toilet is situated next to the entrance door and a sliding door completely isolates it from the central living space.

To obtain harmony in the apartment, the furnishings were carefully selected. On one of the lateral walls, a piece of IKEA furniture unites the entire space, from the kitchen/dining room to the living room. As a result, the kitchen is integrated with the living room, creating a warmer environment. In the living area, Pla exposed a brick wall and managed to establish the room's independence with a sofa from Pilma/Dom. The dining room table and lighting, also from Pilma/Dom, contributes to the warmth of the space, as does the wood floor.

By studying the placement of the pieces and furnishings that make up the residence, the interior designer achieved a functional and modern renovation that floods a remarkable, diaphanous space with light.

A BOX FOR THE SHOWER

To incorporate the shower into the center of the space, it was necessary to use a piece of furniture that divided the two areas of the residence. A small staircase leads up to the shower, and the new installations are hidden underneath this platform, which also adds the sensation of an element placed on top of the original floor.

Light colors, used for the furnishings, the hardwood floors, and the kitchen cabinets, create a uniform and spacious atmosphere in the entryway.

The details of the shower, like the lamp and the simple geometric lines of the towel bar, reinforce the formality of the exterior box.

Loft in an Attic

Manuel Ocaña del Valle

Madrid, Spain | 376 sq. feet | Photographs by Luis Asín

☐ What is now a comfortable, modern residence was once a small, 323-square-foot space, unsuitable for living. Located in a 150-year-old building in the up-and-coming Madrid neighborhood of Chueca, the loft provides many uses resolved in unitary and flexible spaces. The furnishings were designed as part of the architecture itself, in order to make the most of every available space.

To expand the residence's usable surface area, the architect took advantage of the 15-foot-high ceilings. Under the inclined roofs, in the tallest part of the space, he divided the area into two floors, which increased the surface area by 91 square feet. The number of rooms in the loft is extensive, especially given the limited space available. The lower floor includes a dressing room, living room, dining room, kitchen, bathroom, and terrace, while the loft contains a bedroom, bathroom, dressing room, and laundry room. To optimize the space, it was necessary to conduct a rigorous study in order to take advantage of every square foot. The result is a playful exploration of the home that avoids tradi-tional, rigid models. This strategy emphasizes functional flexibility. When the residents want to eat, the entire loft is a dining room; when they want to sit down, the entire space transforms into a living room; and when they want to sleep, the entire apartment is a bedroom. Technical rigor and constructional exactitude were the tools used to resolve certain aspects of the project. The apartment is located in a dirty, noisy, and disorganized urban quarter, so the project aimed to get rid of the landscape noise in order to create a peaceful home. To this end, the architect proposed a "noise damp-ener" in the form of a transitional space where the city-to-residence shift takes place. This versatile area is a directional wood box that connects the interior and the exterior. A folding glass closure divides the space into two parts. The exterior banister also demarcates the residence, protecting it from the noise of the city. The furnishings are compact and integrated into the architecture. A closet is located under the staircase, and the kitchen and bathroom on the ground floor are grouped together so the rest of the space can remain open.

THE COLOR WHITE

Starting with the wooden box on the terrace, everything was painted white in an attempt to instill the space with a sense of calm and to amplify the feeling of spaciousness. The furnishings, also in white, emphasize this concept and merge with the interior architecture.

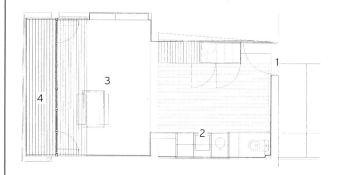

Ground floor plan

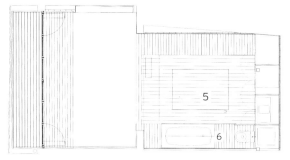

Attic floor plan

1. Access
2. Kitchen
3. Dining room
4. Terrace
5. Bedroom
6. Bathroom

The wooden terrace extends into the interior, producing a platform that can be used as a sofa or chair. This clever detail integrates the balcony and opens the interior space by extending it to the wooden banister.

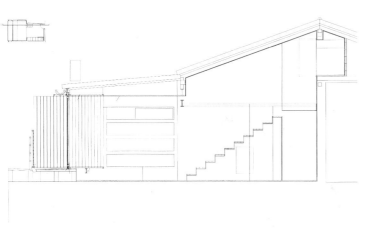

Longitudinal sections

In the attic, the loft is separated from the bedroom by a matted, white glass screen that does not reach the ceiling or floor. This gives the space the same flexibility and amplitude as the rest of the apartment.

Minimum and Austere

Sandra Aparicio & Ignacio Forteza

Barcelona, Spain | 376 sq. feet | Photographs by Eugeni Pons

☐ The renovation of this small apartment was designed for a client who lives in the country, but needs a space to spend the night in the city. The project entailed creating an apartment that carefully covers the basic functions with minimal elements.

In order to amplify the space, the designers tore down all the partition walls and created a single room that includes the living area, the dining table, and the bedroom. The different atmospheres were created through the placement of the furniture. In the open space, with reduced dimensions, the designers separated the bedroom from the living room with a piece of furniture that contains the television and also serves as the dining table. Made out of DM (wood) lacquered in white and with stainless steel feet, the piece articulates the two ambiences, maintaining an

aspect of amplitude. A low shelf, also made of DM, supports the stereo and books. The bed, designed specially for this space, is made of beechwood with a natural varnish on an iron structure. Since it has larger dimensions than the mattress, it also functions as a night table, supporting books and a lamp. A sofa, at the other end of the room, is Perobell's "Metropolitan" model.

The service zones—the bathroom, the dressing room, and interior patio—are accessible from the bedroom area. The kitchen, custom-made in white Formica, is reached via a screen of transparent glass that isolates the kitchen from the living area while amplifying the space. In this way, the space is divided into two rectangles: one without dividers that contains the living area and bedroom, and a fragmented one that contains the services.

A natural color palette is used throughout the apartment and the furnishings to accentuate the unity of the space.

WHITE TABLE

The table serves different functions in a very subtle way: it is a dining table, desk, and a place for the television and books. Its clean lines and smooth, white finish make it barely perceptible inside the space. This solution accentuates the integration of the entire ambience.

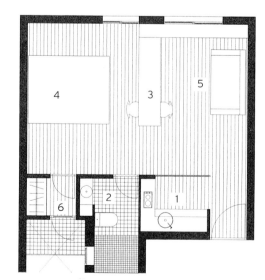

Floor plan

1. Kitchen
2. Bathroom
3. Table
4. Bedroom
5. Living room
6. Closet

The security glass that separates the living room from the kitchen is supported by a stainless steel frame with a minimal section, which emphasizes the element's lightness and the relationship between the two rooms.

Everything in a Cabinet

Guillaume Terver & Fabienne Couvert

Paris, France | 322 sq. feet | Photographs by Vincent Leroux/ACI Roca-Sastre

☐ Years ago, this small apartment formed part of a building that housed a religious congregation. Architects Guillaume Terver and Fabienne Couvert preserved only pieces that reminded them of the space's original character: the entrance door, the chimney, and the bathroom. The 322-sq.-foot studio combines the space's classic, original elements with innovative technical and functional solutions that are grouped in a single object: a cabinet.

This loft in Paris centers on a single piece of furniture that contains all the elements necessary for a pleasant living space. It consists of a square, wooden box on which the architects secured sycamore panels. All the various components of the residence are contained in the box: the bed in the upper part, a door underneath that leads to the kitchen, a closet at the end, and a glass space for the television. Next to the TV, a folding table functions as a desk and computer station. The printer, stereo, and fax are stored in a closet next to it. The ventilation ducts are installed in the façade, and the electrical and water installations are hidden underneath the floor. By painting some parts in red, orange, or blue—as if they

were pieces of a puzzle—the architects managed to accentuate the uniqueness of the sycamore cabinet, which contains everything that the apartment needs.

Even though the space was small to begin with, the 32-sq.-foot ceilings permitted the bed to be elevated, assuring a sufficient distance between the mattress and the ceiling. The bed, which is reached via a staircase stored in the cabinet, is attached to a small blue wall that serves as a night table and that corresponds to the kitchen ceiling. So that all spaces can enjoy natural light, the various pieces that make up the cabinet do not touch the ceiling, allowing light to flow throughout. The simplicity of the kitchen follows the same clear and functional design: a stainless steel refrigerator and stove, with certain touches of color to break its sobriety. In the corner of the room is a more relaxed space that contrasts with the straight lines created by the chimney, the library, and the CD storage units.

The strategy behind this project allows the space to conserve its original proportions and character. It takes full advantage of the light granted by the two windows in order to create a spacious ambience in only 322 sq. feet.

The lower part of the bed houses the closet, in which the architects incorporated invisible hinges that give it a continual and uniform exterior image.

GROUPING

The placement of all the components of the residence in the same object makes this project a technical and functional exercise. Each piece is carefully situated to make the most of every inch while establishing a coherent relationship with the exterior.

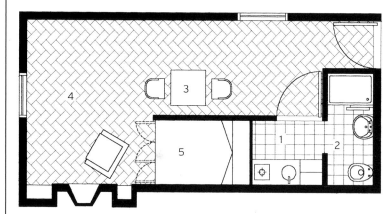

Floor plan

1. Kitchen
2. Bathroom
3. Dining room
4. Living room
5. Bedroom

The contrast between the elements preserved from the original space, like the chimney and the windows, enriches the atmosphere and makes it dynamic.

Light and Dark

Karin Léopold & François Fauconnet

Paris, France | 322 sq. feet | Photographs by Vicent Leroux/ACI Roca Sastre

☐ This old apartment, located in a traditional residential building in Paris, consisted of a small, subdivided attic that was in a state of disrepair. The roof features the pronounced incline so typical of the top floor of a Parisian building, and the windows offer splendid views of the city and the Eiffel Tower. The apartment's restoration included incorporating the interior's charming elements while freeing the space of the cramped sensation of only 322 sq. feet.

The architects Karin Léopold and François Fauconnet decided to knock down the walls and the false ceiling and expose the beams to gain height and the feeling of a loft. They organized the project around a cabinet in which they grouped the toilet, the heating system, shelves, and the entrance door, which became one more component of this innovative object. The kitchen is situated at one extreme of the cabinet, and the shower is found on the other and separated from the space with white, matte glass. The bathroom, the kitchen, and electrical and water installations are grouped in the middle of the cabinet, which runs along one of the lateral walls.

The architects´ idea was to provide all the elements that are indispensable for comfort without dividing the space. Instead of using a partition wall, they delimited the bathroom with a glass wall and the dark wooden headboard of the bed. In order to make the most of every inch in the kitchen, the oven is integrated into the wood façade and the English slate counter is custom-made. The counter's function is twofold: it acts as a shelf and as a support for the kitchen fixtures, designed by the Dane Arne Jacobsen, and it centralizes the electrical and water installations. The architects also used slate for the cabinets of the kitchen and bathroom. For the floor, they used dark-colored parquet. Other details, including the furnishings, the tablecloths created by Kim and Garo, and the Chinese dishes, contribute to the apartment's charm. Another key feature of this project comes from the contrast of the white walls with the various objects made of dark wood.

The architects managed to liberate the space and to clear the windows. They respected the space's original character yet managed to create a traditional residence within it.

CABINET

Grouping the services and the entrance inside a cabinet that crosses the entire space in a longitudinal sense unified the residence and avoided the need for interior divisions. The interior of this element is carefully designed to establish a proper working order within a minimal width.

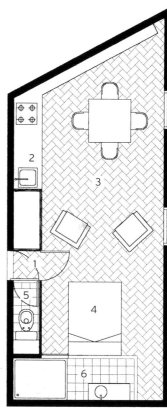

Floor plan

1. Access
2. Kitchen
3. Dining room
4. Bedroom
5. Bathroom
6. Bathroom

The Vola fixture, by designer Arne Jacobsen, was used in the kitchen, in the bathroom, and in the shower, thus becoming part of the decoration of the general space.

The lighting, by means of small reflectors suspended from the ceiling and walls, emphasizes the contrast between the materials and creates the effect of depth.

Playful and Intimate

Gary Chang/EDGE (HK) Ltd.

Hong Kong, China | 323 sq. feet | Photographs by Almond Chu

☐ This apartment, located on the east island of Hong Kong, was designed by Gary Chang as his personal residence. Located in a popular neighborhood, this old flat was previously the home of a large family. The goal of the project was to create a space that, despite its reduced proportions, contains all the necessary residential functions, yet has flexibility for rest and leisure.

In order to make the most of the principal window located in the back part of the residence, the architect grouped the bathroom, kitchen, and laundry room in the front. As a result, the main space could enjoy the window, the best source of natural light. As an empty space, it could also accommodate diverse uses as the bedroom, living room, study, and video room. To achieve flexibility in such a small area, Chang combined light divisions, carefully planned lighting, and mobile furnishings. All his possessions for work and leisure, such as books, videos, and disks, as well as the home's accessories and the closet, are stored in a system of metallic shelves that are discreetly hidden behind white curtains. The result is that the central space can accommodate all the daytime and nighttime activities with the simple movement of one or several curtains. The architect used transparent and white translucent materials. By combining them with mood lighting, he gave the apartment a quality of lightness in which the materials seem to vanish. To tone down the rigidity of the floor and make it more ethereal, Chang and his collaborators used fluorescent tubes on one side and a more brilliant light that articulates the structural parts on the other. The only heavy object, at least in appearance, is the solid-cherry-wood tower that contains the projector, the refrigerator, the kitchen, the bathroom, and the washing machine. Each detail was carefully thought out and designed with the objective of making the most of every corner of this 323-sq.-foot space. In this single atmosphere, the architect managed to group residential neccesities in a simple and elegant way. The lights and the convertible elements alter the apartment for different circumstances, adding a playful yet relaxed spirit.

The kitchen cabinets and appliances are contained in a single wooden cabinet found near the entrance. The top shelves, hidden behind the curtains, are suspended from the wall. The lower shelves are supported by a fine metallic structure that complements the lightness of the space.

PROJECTION

The small proportions of this space seem to vanish thanks to the layout, which faces the back window. At times, the space has the atmosphere of a small cinema. The apartment turns into a platform from which to contemplate the urban landscape or to watch a film.

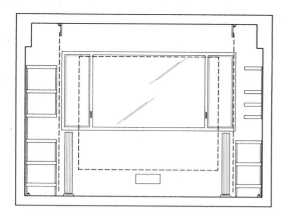

Transversal section of the living room

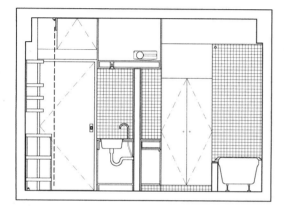

Transversal section of the bathroom and kitchen

Despite the small space, the architect achieved great formal expressiveness in the bathroom. This space combines design elements, like fixtures by Philippe Starck, with economical solutions such as lighting from two fluorescent tubes.

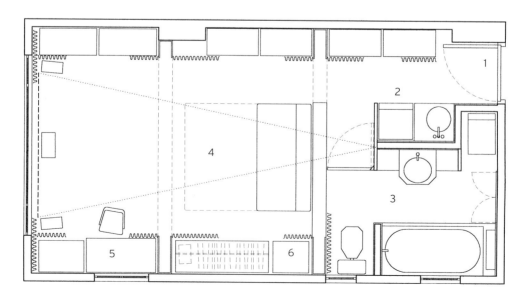

Floor Plan

1. Access
2. Kitchen
3. Bathroom
4. Living room and bedroom
5. Studio
6. Cabinet

The placement of each piece of furniture breaks traditional schemes and produces diverse spatial relationships in the same atmosphere.

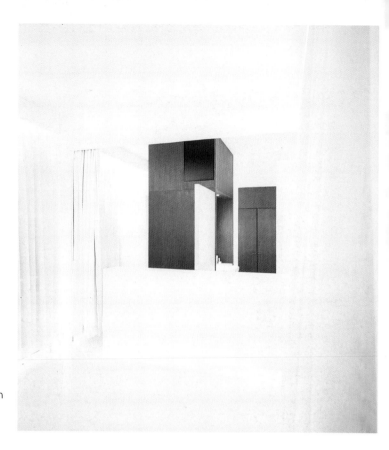

The dark wood cabinet that contains the kitchen appliances and the bathroom stands out as a sculpture in an atmosphere dominated by the color white.

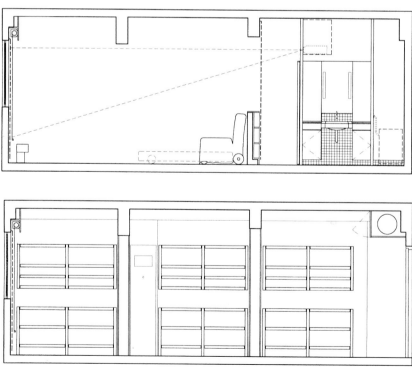

Longitudinal sections

Functional Folds

Stéphane Chamard

Paris, France | 172 sq. feet | Photographs by Vincent Leroux/ACI Roca-Sastre

☐ At the back of a patio in the sixth district of Paris, a city renowned for its small living spaces, is this old, 172-sq.-foot doorman's room. The young architect, Stéphane Chamard, transformed the tiny quarters into a luminous interior in which to live and work. The area consists of a cubic space with high ceilings, which permitted the architect to create two floors. Chamard used every last inch, making the most of the room and its openings by giving them a functional character.

The main feature of the apartment is the staircase that the architect designed to unite the two levels. This structure, made of folded metal and later lacquered in white, determines the layout. Each step is 10 inches high to create a minimum number of folds and to keep the staircase in the smallest space possible. The staircase's light and graphic form rests on a box that contains the television and that also serves as a kitchen sideboard. The entire space is centered around the box, which manages to be solid yet light, like a sheet of folded paper. The enormous windows are separated to bathe both floors with light. The luminosity accentuates the feeling of spaciousness that the

architect created in this small apartment.

On the bottom level, the architect installed a kitchen equipped with shelves and disguised by a panel of pleated laminates that isolates it from the living room and the dining room. The selection of designer furnishings also helps create the impression of a homogeneous space. The setting includes a palm leaf table that was found on the street and two armchairs designed by Charles Eames. The architect used painted cement for the floor, covered with courtide.

In order to take full advantage of the possibilities on the upper level, the architect devised a space under the desk in which to store the cotton mattress during the day. The bookcase in front of the desk, made of a suspended box of wood and glass, defines the room. There is storage room for documents underneath the bookcase. The curtains are made of Nepalese paper, and the floor features large sheets of wood finished with white lacquer. The bathroom is also found on the upper level. In little more than 21.5 sq. feet, it includes the toilet, the shower, and the sink. The bathroom fixtures are mounted on the wall.

METALLIC SHEET

The lightest way to produce the staircase, both structurally and aesthetically, was to use a bent metallic sheet. A self-bearing structure, the staircase enriches the space with its sculptural character that is solid yet light.

Upper floor plan

Ground floor plan

1. Kitchen
2. Bathroom
3. Dining room
4. Bedroom/studio

The design of the furnishings, adjusted to the size and configuration of the project, was essential for making the most of this space's minimal proportions. The work desk also functions as a shelf, as a banister, and as a space to store the cotton mattress.